Picture the Bible

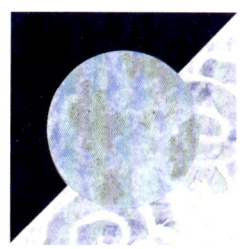    

STACY JOHNSON MYERS

featuring the private art collection of First Congregational Church

the Pilgrim Press
since 1640

The Pilgrim Press, 700 Prospect Avenue East
Cleveland, Ohio 44115-1100
thepilgrimpress.com

© 2021 First Congregational United Church of Christ of River Falls, WI, and Stacy Johnson Myers

All right reserved. No part of this book may be used or reproduced in any manner whatsoever without written permission.

Published 2021 by The Pilgrim Press

25 24 23 22 21   1 2 3 4 5

Library of Congress Control Number: 2021932619

ISBN 978-0-8298-2117-8 (alk. paper)
ISBN 978-0-8298-2118-5 (ebook)

Printed in China

To my beloved children
Andrew, Matthew, and Kathryn Elizabeth
&
To all the children of
First Congregational Church

Contents

Come, Picture the Bible!	1
God Makes the World	3
Adam and Eve in the Garden	4
Jealousy and Murder	6
The Big Flood	9
God's Promise to Abraham and Sarah	11
Joseph and His Brothers	12
Living in Slavery	15
Baby Moses	17
God Speaks to Moses	19
The Passover	21
Fleeing from Egypt	22
The Ten Commandments	24
A New Homeland	26
God Chooses David	28
King Solomon's Temple	31
Naaman is Healed	33
Sent Away to Babylon	34
Daniel and the Lions	36
Jonah and the Big Fish	39
Isaiah's Message	40
God Chooses Mary	43
Jesus Is Born	45
The Magi Visit Jesus	46
The Flight to Egypt	49
Jesus Teaches in the Temple	51
John Baptizes People	52
Jesus Is Baptized	55
The Devil Tempts Jesus	57
Jesus Calls Followers	58
Jesus Performs a Miracle in Cana	61
Jesus Heals a Man	63
Jesus Preaches on a Mountain	64
Jesus Tells Stories	66
Jesus Blesses Children	68
Transfiguration	71

Mary and Martha Learn from Jesus	73
Jesus Talks with a Samaritan Woman	74
Jesus Feeds a Crowd	77
Zacchaeus Meets Jesus	78
The Parade into Jerusalem	81
Jesus Turns over Tables	82
One Last Supper	84
Jesus Washes the Disciples' Feet	87
Jesus Prays in a Garden	89
Jesus Is Betrayed and Arrested	90
The Crucifixion	93
The Women Visit the Tomb	94
A Walk to Emmaus	96
Thomas Sees Jesus	99
Jesus Goes to Heaven	100
The Pentecost Celebration	102
People of the Way: Let Justice Roll	104
A Note to Adults	106

Come, Picture the Bible!

The Bible is filled with stories and ideas that show us who God is and what God is like. The first words of the Bible are, "In the beginning," and the last word is "Amen." In between those words are all kinds of stories: long stories, short stories, scary stories, funny stories, confusing stories, and comforting stories—and all of them are about God. Even though these stories are much older than you are, they are still your stories because you belong to God.

God Makes the World

In the beginning there was only God and nothing else.

Then God said, "Let there be light!" and there was light. God called the light "Day," and God called the darkness "Night." That was the first day.

God said, "Let there be heavens that are separate from waters." God called the heavens "Sky." That was the second day.

God said, "Let the waters come together so there can also be dry land." God called the land "Earth" and the water "Seas." Then God said, "Let there be plants and seeds, and all kinds of fruits." God saw that it was all good. That was the third day.

God said, "Let there be lights: one for the day and another for the night." So, the sun shines in the day, and the stars and moon shine in the night. God saw that it was good. That was the fourth day.

God said, "Let there be creatures in the waters, and birds in the sky." God saw these were good. That was the fifth day.

God said, "Let the land be filled with all kinds of animals, from the tallest giraffes to the tiniest ladybugs. And let us make people who show God." God looked at the whole creation and said, "Yes, it is all very good!" That was the sixth day.

After creating the world, God rested on the seventh day.

Make a list of the tiniest things you can think of that God made. Make a list of the most gigantic things you can think of that God made.

Genesis 1:1-2:2

Adam and Eve in the Garden

When God made people, they were named Adam (which means "earthling") and Eve (which means "living").

Adam and Eve lived in a garden called Eden. The garden had everything they needed; it was perfect for them. God asked the people to help take care of the garden. God also said, "You may eat fruit from all trees in Eden, but don't eat fruit from the tree in the middle of the garden."

One day a serpent, who was being tricky, told Eve that if she ate the fruit from the middle tree she would be like God. Adam and Eve decided to eat some of the fruit God told them not to eat.

Later that day, God came to visit Adam and Eve. God called out, "Where are you?" Adam answered, "I'm hiding because I'm afraid." God said, "Did you eat fruit from the tree in the middle of the garden?" Adam answered, "Eve tricked me." Eve said, "The serpent tricked me."

After that, Adam and Eve had to leave the garden. Life became much more difficult, as it does when people disobey God.

God asks people to take care of the world. How do you take care of people? How do you take care of nature?

Genesis 2:4-23
Genesis 3:1-19

Jealousy and Murder

Adam and Eve had three sons. Cain was the oldest, then Abel, and the youngest was Seth.

Abel was a shepherd and took care of sheep. Cain was a farmer and planted seeds.

Cain and Abel each gave a gift to God from their work. Abel gave a lamb and Cain gave grain from his fields. God liked Abel's offering and turned away Cain's offering. This made Cain very angry and jealous of Abel.

God said to Cain, "Why do you look angry? Do the right thing. Don't let your anger take over your life."

Cain said to Abel, "Let's go for a walk." On their walk, Cain killed Abel. This was a terrible thing to do. People are supposed to take care of each other, not hurt them.

God asked Cain, "Where is your brother Abel?" Cain lied, "I do not know. Am I in charge of my brother?" God punished Cain and said that Cain had to wander and never belong anywhere. Cain said, "That punishment is too much! Anyone who finds me will kill me!" God said, "No, that will not happen. I will protect you so no one tries to kill you." Cain left and went to a land called Nod, which means Wandering.

What makes you jealous? How do you try to do the right thing when you are angry?

Genesis 4:1-16
Genesis 4:25

The Big Flood

In those days, many people were hurting each other and stealing from each other. God was angry about people's choices. God wanted to wash away everything that was evil and wrong in the world.

Noah was a good man who listened to God and didn't harm others. God told Noah to build a very large wooden boat, called an "ark." Noah and his family and two of every kind of creature went into the ark.

Then God sent the rain, lots of rain. It rained and rained for forty days and forty nights. Everything was flooded! When the rain ended, it took many days for the earth to dry.

Noah sent a dove to fly over the land. When the dove returned with an olive leaf, Noah knew the land was drying. Seven days later, Noah sent out the dove again, but this time the dove did not return. Noah knew the dove had found a place to build a nest, so Noah and his family and all the animals left the ark in order to build their homes too.

Then God promised Noah, "Never again will a flood destroy the earth." God put a rainbow above the clouds. "When I see this rainbow," God said, "I will remember my promise." Noah and his family remembered God's promise too.

Which of God's creatures are your favorites?
Name the type of home each creature has.

Genesis 6:5-9:17

God's Promise to Abraham and Sarah

Long after the flood, many people still thought they didn't need God, but God never gave up on them. God noticed a man named Abram and his wife Sarai. They didn't always live as God wanted, but when they made mistakes, they changed how they lived. This is what faithful people do.

God chose Abram and Sarai to show others how to live in God's way. God gave Abram and Sarai three promises: they would have their own homeland; they would have as many people in their family as stars in the sky; and they would be a blessing to others. These promises surprised Abram and Sarai, because they didn't live in their own country and they didn't have any children.

God told them, "To show you that I will keep my promises, I will change your names. You are now Abraham and Sarah. I will always be your God, and you will always be my special people."

Abraham and Sarah moved to many different places, and they did not have any children. They wondered if God forgot the three promises. Finally, one day, some visitors came with a message from God. They said, "Sarah is going to have a baby." It was so unbelievable that Sarah laughed right out loud. She was too old to have a baby! But soon Sarah became pregnant and had a baby. They named him Isaac. Isaac brought great joy and showed his parents that God's promises are true.

> A "blessing" is someone or something that shows God's love and brings people joy. What can you do to be a blessing to someone today?

Genesis 17:1-27
Genesis 18:1-15
Genesis 21:1-8

Joseph and His Brothers

Abraham and Sarah had a son named Isaac. When Isaac grew up, he had a son named Jacob. When Jacob grew up, he had twelve sons and one of his sons was named Joseph.

When Joseph was 17 years old, his father Jacob gave him a bright and colorful coat. Joseph's brothers were very jealous. The brothers also did not like hearing about Joseph's dreams. In those dreams, Joseph was quite important, and all the brothers had to bow down to him.

One day Joseph's brothers had enough. They grabbed Joseph, took his fancy coat, and sold him to travelers who were going to Egypt. Then the brothers lied to their father Jacob and said that Joseph had been killed.

In Egypt, times were hard for Joseph, but he kept dreaming. The hard days turned into days with new chances. Joseph became an assistant to Egypt's king, called the Pharaoh, and Joseph led Egypt through a famine. Joseph was a hero!

Back home, Jacob's family was hungry because of the famine. The brothers went to Egypt for food. They did not recognize Joseph, but Joseph knew them. Joseph told them, "You hurt me, but God made something good after the hard days." The brothers returned home to get their father Jacob and their families, and they all went to live in Egypt.

"Forgiveness" happens when we stop feeling angry at someone who hurt us. Why do you think Joseph forgave his brothers? Who has forgiven you?

Genesis 37
Genesis 39-45

Living in Slavery

Jacob's family lived in Egypt for a very long time. They were called "Israelites," because God had given Jacob the name "Israel." The Egyptians called them "Hebrews." The people lived in Egypt so long that eventually there was a new Pharaoh.

Pharaoh saw how many Israelites lived in Egypt. He worried they would take over and become more powerful than he was, or even rebel against him. So Pharaoh of Egypt forced the people to work as slaves. Day after day, they made bricks to build cities. They worked in Egypt's fields. The work was hard, and the people were treated cruelly.

Pharaoh made it hard for the Israelites to be safe. He gave a terrible order to the women who helped Israelite mothers give birth. "Kill the baby if it's a boy," he said, "but the baby can live if it's a girl." Two women refused to follow Pharaoh's order; their names were Shiphrah and Puah.

So Pharaoh gave an order to his soldiers, "Throw every Hebrew baby boy into the Nile River to drown." The Israelites were angry and frightened. They cried out to God for help. They wondered if God had forgotten the promises God made to their ancestors, Sarah and Abraham.

Shiphrah and Puah were brave. What makes it hard to be brave? Why is it important to be brave?

Exodus 1:1-22

Baby Moses

During the terrible years of slavery in Egypt, a woman named Jochebed had a baby boy. She loved her baby and made a plan to protect him from Pharaoh's order. She wove a basket and gently laid her baby in it. Jochebed then put the basket in the water at the edge of the Nile River. Jochebed's daughter, Miriam, hid along the river where she could watch the basket and keep it safe.

Pharaoh's daughter, a princess, came to the Nile to bathe. She saw the basket along the edge and heard the baby cry. The princess told her servant to fetch the basket. Then she looked inside the basket and felt sorry for the baby boy.

Miriam, who had been watching, said, "I know someone who could feed and take care of him for you." The princess agreed.

Miriam brought her mother to Pharaoh's daughter, who did not know that Jochebed was the baby's own mother. The princess offered to pay Jochebed to take care of the baby. Pharaoh's daughter named the baby Moses.

When Moses was older, Jochebed brought him to Pharaoh's daughter, who adopted him as her son.

> Moses had a birth mom, an adoptive mom, a sister, and many more people who took care of him.
> Who are the people taking care of you?

Exodus 2:1-10

God Speaks to Moses

Moses lived in Pharaoh's house as part of the royal family, but because his birth mother Jochebed had raised him, Moses also knew what life was like for the Israelites in slavery.

When Moses grew up, he sometimes went to see the Israelites making bricks for cities and plowing fields. Often the Egyptians were cruel to the people. This made Moses very upset. Once when Moses saw an Egyptian hurting an Israelite man, Moses killed the Egyptian. Moses knew the Pharaoh would be angry when he discovered what he had done, so he fled to the desert. There he became a shepherd, taking care of sheep.

One day Moses was taking care of the sheep and saw something strange: a bush was on fire, but it was not burning up. Then something even stranger happened. Moses heard God call his name from the bush, saying, "Moses! Moses!" Moses answered, "I'm here." God said, "Take off your sandals. You are on holy ground." Moses was afraid, but God continued. "My people are suffering. Pharaoh says they are slaves and have to make bricks. Lead them out of Egypt. Tell Pharaoh to let my people go!"

Moses didn't want to do God's work. He thought he didn't speak well enough to talk to Pharaoh. But God insisted. Finally, with his brother Aaron's help, Moses went to Pharaoh and announced, "God said, 'Let my people go!'"

Imagine God telling you something important. How would you feel? What would you think?

Exodus 2:11-4:17

The Passover

Pharaoh didn't want to let the Israelites go. He said to Moses and Aaron, "I don't know your God. I'm not letting the people go!" Then Pharaoh made the Israelites work even harder. Moses and Aaron tried again. They told Pharaoh, "God said, 'Let my people go!'" Again Pharaoh said, "No!"

Moses was frustrated. He complained, "God, this isn't working. Things are getting worse for your people, and you aren't doing anything to help." God answered, "Watch what I am going to do to Pharaoh." Then mysterious things began to happen in Egypt. One day, there were frogs everywhere. Another day, flies swarmed all over the camels and cows. Then the river changed and looked like blood. God sent a plague of locusts and another plague of lice. God made hail fall, and God made the day look like night. Nothing worked to change Pharaoh's mind.

Finally, God told Moses there would be one last plague—a plague of death. The oldest sons in every family would die. Moses told the Israelites to slaughter a lamb to eat that night, and to paint blood from the lamb on their door posts. The blood was a signal for death to pass over their homes. They did what Moses told them, and their sons did not die. Everywhere in Egypt, people were crying. During the night, Pharaoh called Moses and Aaron and said, "Go away! Leave my land! Take everything and go!"

> Moses trusted God and the people trusted Moses.
> Who do you trust?

Exodus 5-12

Fleeing from Egypt

When Pharaoh said, "Go!" the Israelites left Egypt in a hurry. They left so quickly that they baked their bread before it had risen, and it stayed flat. They wanted to get away from Egypt and Pharaoh and find the land God promised long ago to Sarah and Abraham.

The Israelites traveled as far as the edge of the Red Sea, but back in Egypt, Pharaoh changed his mind. He wanted to force the Israelites to come back and work. Pharaoh sent horses, riders, and chariots to chase and capture the people. The people were trapped. In front of them was the sea, and behind them was Pharaoh's army coming to capture them. There was no way out until God made one.

God helped Moses make a dry path through the sea so the people could walk across safely. As soon as the Israelites were on the other side, the Red Sea filled up again and Pharaoh's army drowned. The Israelites were safe! They celebrated, singing and dancing for joy while Miriam, Moses' sister, played a tambourine. The people never forgot that God saved them.

The Israelites didn't know where to find the land God promised to them, but God stayed with them, day and night. During the day, the people followed a thick cloud and at night they followed a glowing fire.

What does it feel like to be safe?

Exodus 13:17-15:21

The Ten Commandments

Life was hard on the journey away from Egypt. The Israelites didn't have much food or water. The land was unfamiliar. Before long, the people started to complain, but God was with them. When the people were hungry, God gave them special food like bread, called manna, and quails to eat. When they were thirsty, God told Moses to hit his staff on a rock and water spurted out!

Along the way, the people camped at the bottom of a mountain called Sinai. On the third morning there, the people woke up to loud thunder, lightning, even a trumpet blast. They were afraid, but Moses knew it was God. God told Moses to go to the top of the mountain. God gave Moses ten commandments—ten rules about how to treat God and one another—and carved them onto two flat stones. The Ten Commandments said:

> I am God • Don't make anything more important than God • God's name is special; don't use it to hurt others • Remember to observe a rest day • Show love and respect to your parents and the people who take care of you • Protect others; never murder • Adults, be faithful in marriage • Don't take things that aren't yours • Always tell the truth • Be happy with what you have.

These commandments became part of Israel's Torah, or teachings, about how to live in God's way.

Which commandments are about how you treat God?
Which commandments are about how you treat others?

Exodus 16 •
Exodus 17:1-6 •
Exodus 19-20 •
Deuteronomy 5:1-22

A New Homeland

The Israelites left Mount Sinai and wandered in a desert wilderness to get to the land God promised them. They carried the two stone tablets with them, because they knew God's commandments were important. God told Moses to make a special tent where people could worship and feel close to God. Builders made a beautiful box, called the Ark of the Covenant, to store the stone tablets with the Ten Commandments. As the people traveled, they carried the Ark and brought the tent with them so God would always be close to the people.

Finally, after forty long years, the Israelites came to the land that God promised Sarah and Abraham. Before they entered the land, Moses stood in front of the people and said, "Today you have a choice to make. If you follow God's way, you will live well. If you don't follow God's way, you will not live long. Choose life!"

Then Moses stood on Mount Nebo and looked over their new homeland, which was called Canaan. It was beautiful! After seeing it with his eyes, Moses, who was very old, died. Joshua took Moses' place as leader of the people.

Pretend you are Moses standing on Mount Nebo.
What do you see? What do you hear? How do you feel?

Exodus 25:1-22
Deuteronomy 30:11-31:3
Deuteronomy 34

God Chooses David

Life in Canaan was very good, but sometimes it was hard too. Other people already lived there, and they didn't always get along with the Israelites. What should the people do? Joshua continued to lead the people by listening to God. Other leaders and teachers and priests helped the Israelites settle into their new home in Canaan, with God as their most important leader. They called their homeland Israel, which means "saved by God."

After many years, the Israelites wanted to have a king who could make them a powerful nation. God warned them that human leaders, no matter how great, could also be selfish. The people wouldn't listen. They still wanted a king.

God named Saul as the first king. At first Saul was faithful, but then he stopped following God's way. Israel needed a different king, so God asked a priest named Samuel to help choose the next king. Samuel visited Jesse who had seven sons. God chose David, the youngest son, to be Israel's next king. To show he was God's choice, Samuel dripped oil on David's head from a ram's horn. David was young, but God knew he could do important things.

What important things can you do?

1 Samuel 16:1-13

King Solomon's Temple

David ruled Israel for forty years. He was a great king, but he also made mistakes. When he made mistakes, he changed his ways, he repented, and tried again to be faithful to God. When David died, his son Solomon became king. Solomon was known far and wide as a wise king.

In those days, the people worshipped God in a tent, called a tabernacle, just as they did after they left Egypt and wandered in the wilderness to find a new home. Solomon remembered that his father, David, wanted to build a temple for God—a beautiful place to worship. God didn't need a fancy house to live in, because God was wherever the people were, but after a while God agreed. It took seven years for Solomon's workers to build a gigantic, magnificent, sparkly temple.

When the temple was done, Solomon prayed, "God of Israel, there is no other god like you! You never forget the promises you make to your people. There is not enough room in all heaven or earth for you. You will not only live in this temple, but please listen to your people when we pray and forgive our sins." For a long, long time the temple was very important to Israel. People worshipped, prayed, and gave offerings to God at the temple.

Solomon wanted a magnificent temple for God.
Describe the kind of worship place you think is right for God.

1 Kings 5-6
1 Kings 8:22-30

Naaman Is Healed

Elisha was a prophet. He gave people messages from God and he did miraculous things, because God was with him.

In a country called Aram, far from Israel where Elisha lived, there was a powerful man named Naaman. Naaman had leprosy, a disease that left sore spots on his skin. Nothing healed the sores. One of the servants in Naaman's house was a young girl from Israel who knew about Elisha. She said, "Naaman should go to my hometown. There is a prophet who could cure him."

When Naaman had permission from the king, he left for Israel and took chariots, horses, silver, gold, and fancy clothes with him as gifts to anyone who could heal him. Elisha heard about Naaman coming to Israel and invited him to his home. When Naaman arrived, a messenger from Elisha instructed him, "Go wash in the Jordan River seven times. Then you will be healed."

Naaman was really mad. "We have rivers at home! I could have taken a bath in a river there!" But Naaman's servants said, "If the prophet asked you to do something hard, you would have done it. This is an easy thing to do." So Naaman washed in the Jordan River seven times. When he came out, his skin was smooth. He was healed! Naaman said, "Now I know the God of Israel is the greatest of all!"

Why would someone not do something easy even though it is important?

2 Kings 5:1-19

Sent Away to Babylon

As Solomon grew older, he stopped being a faithful king. When Solomon's son Rehoboam was king, he was cruel to the people. Times were tough in Israel. God needed to help Israel, so God chose people to be "prophets" to give messages from God to the people. The prophets told Israel, "Stop hurting people. Take care of others. Always be fair. Don't be selfish. Help the poor." Some people listened. Others did not.

The prophets continued to warn people, but still Israel turned from God's way. Before long, the kingdom divided into two parts because the people could not get along with each other. One kingdom was still called Israel and the other was called Judah.

Soldiers from another country came and took over Israel. Not long after Israel was destroyed, and more soldiers made the people in Judah leave their land. Now God's people were in exile—they lived in a country that was not their own. The country was called Babylon. The people were miserable because they didn't want to live, sing, or pray in Babylon. They wanted to be home in Israel. Many people wondered if God had forgotten them.

When have you been lonely or felt forgotten?

Jeremiah 52
Psalm 137

Daniel and the Lions

Daniel was one of God's people who lived in exile in Babylon, but Daniel did not forget God. He prayed three times each day.

The King of Babylon, named Darius, knew Daniel was wise and trustworthy. King Darius made Daniel an advisor and often asked him for advice. Some men were jealous of Daniel. They wanted the king to depend on them, so the men tricked King Darius into making a law that said no one could pray to anyone other than King Darius. Anyone who broke the law would be thrown into the den of lions.

Daniel knew about the new law, but he was still prayed to God. The jealous men spied on Daniel and saw him praying to God, so they ran to tell the king. King Darius was upset because he did not want to hurt Daniel, but he had to follow his own law, so he had Daniel arrested and put in the lions' den. King Darius said to Daniel, "May your God save you."

The next morning King Darius rushed to the lions' den. He called out, "Daniel! Has your God saved you?" Daniel answered, "God kept me safe. The lions did not hurt me." King Darius ordered that Daniel be taken out of the den. King Darius said, "I am making a new law. Everyone in my land will worship Daniel's God, the living God, who saved Daniel from the lions!"

Do you think Daniel was courageous or crazy to be faithful to God when it was so dangerous? How so?

Daniel 6

Jonah and the Big Fish

One day God said, "Jonah, go to the city of Nineveh. Tell the people to change their ways. I don't like how they are living." Jonah didn't want to go, so he ran from God and got on a boat sailing far away. While he was on the boat, a great wind came. The boat tossed and turned, and the people were scared. Jonah said, "This terrible wind is my fault. I'm not listening to God. Throw me overboard so the wind stops." So the sailors threw Jonah into the sea, and God sent a big fish that swallowed up Jonah and kept him safe.

Jonah prayed to God from the fish's belly. After three days, the fish threw up Jonah onto the land. God said, "Get up, Jonah. Go to Nineveh. Give them my message." This time Jonah did as God asked. Jonah said, "People of Nineveh! Change your ways!" They listened! Since the people changed, God didn't punish them. But even though God had saved Jonah from the sea, Jonah was angry that God saved the people of Nineveh. He thought God should punish them.

Jonah was fuming and sat down under a bush because the sun was hot. God sent a worm to attack the bush. The bush died and the shade disappeared. Jonah got even angrier. God said, "Jonah! If you care about a bush, surely you understand I care about my people in Nineveh!"

When we get another chance after making a mistake, it is called "grace." Where do you see grace in this story? Have you experienced grace in your life?

Jonah 1-4

Isaiah's Message

Long ago, God's people, Israel, did not live in their own land. First they were nomads, moving from place to place. Then they were forced to be slaves in Egypt. Then for a while lived in the promised land which they said belonged to them. But then the people were captured once again, and they were sent away to live in Babylon. Over time some of them forgot about God's way. Others remembered, but they worried God had forgotten them and the old promises God gave to their ancestors, Sarah and Abraham. They dreamed of being back home in their own land. They wanted to live in God's way. They did not want to be in Babylon.

The people were unhappy and lonely, and many lost hope. But some were hopeful and brave. They remembered God's prophet, Isaiah, who said, "Take comfort! The hard days are over. Prepare! Get ready for what God is doing." Isaiah said God would send a new king who would be a different kind of leader. The new leader would come from King David's family, like a new branch growing from an old tree stump.

Isaiah also said, "Everything will change when we all live in God's way. Lions and lambs will be together and not hurt each other; even children could lead them. Everyone will live in peace." It was a wonderful dream! The people wondered if it could be true. They started to wait for the great new leader.

Is Isaiah's dream completely wild? Wise? Something else? How so?

Isaiah 11:1-9
Isaiah 40

God Chooses Mary

Israel waited a long time for the new leader God promised. The people wondered if the new leader would be great and powerful like King David. They hoped so!

God sent an angel named Gabriel to visit Mary. Mary was young and planned to marry a man named Joseph. Gabriel gave Mary a message from God. Gabriel said, "God chose you! You will have a baby. His name will be Jesus. He will be God's son." Mary was very surprised! She was going to be a mother. Her baby would be the new leader Isaiah talked about. Mary wondered, "How is this possible?" Gabriel answered, "With God, all things are possible."

Mary went to visit her cousin, Elizabeth, who was also pregnant. Elizabeth and her husband, Zechariah, were expecting a baby boy. Elizabeth told Mary, "God blessed you and your baby. Just hearing your voice, the baby inside me leaped for joy."

Mary sang a song to praise God: "My spirit is joyful! God chose me. From now on everyone will know that God blessed me. God's name is special and holy. God emptied out people who think they are powerful and raised up people without power. God gave food to those who are hungry; those who already have enough don't need more. God helped the people of Israel and remembers all promises to their ancestors, Sarah and Abraham."

Imagine you are rich and powerful. What do you hear in Mary's song? Imagine you are hungry. What do you hear?

Luke 1:26-56

Jesus Is Born

In those days, Emperor Augustus was in charge of many lands and people. Emperor Augustus wanted to know how many people lived in his kingdom, so everyone had to go to their hometowns to be counted. Since Joseph was a great-great-great-great-great-great-great-great-great grandson of King David's family, he went to David's city in Judea called Bethlehem. Mary went with Joseph. It was a long trip.

When they got to Bethlehem, the inn was full because so many people had come to be counted. Since there was no place to stay, Joseph and Mary rested with the animals. That night Jesus was born. Mary wrapped her baby tightly in cloth and laid him in a manger, a box for the animals' food.

Outside of Bethlehem, there were shepherds watching their sheep. An angel said to the shepherds, "Don't be afraid, I bring you good news! The leader that God promised, the Messiah, was born! Go to Bethlehem! You will see the baby wrapped up in cloth and lying in a manger." Suddenly many angels burst into the sky and praised God. The angels sang, "Glory to God in the highest and peace to all people on earth!" It was a wonderful, happy night.

Often powerful people hear important news first. Shepherds were not powerful. Why do you think they heard the angels' news first?

Luke 2

The Magi Visit Jesus

When Jesus was born in Bethlehem, Augustus was the emperor and Herod was the king.

In those days, there were wise people—called magi—who studied the stars. The magi noticed a special star in the sky and knew it meant a new king was born. The magi wanted to celebrate the baby and bring him gifts, so they followed the star. When they reached Jerusalem, the magi didn't know where to find the baby, so they asked King Herod, "We are following the star to find the baby who will be a new king. Could you tell us where he is?" Herod was upset. He was the king, not anyone else!

Herod said to the magi, "Go to Bethlehem and search for the baby king there. When you find him, tell me so I can go to worship him too." The magi went to Bethlehem. They found the house where Mary was with the baby. The magi knelt down and worshipped. They gave the baby gifts for a king: gold, frankincense, and myrrh. God warned the magi in a dream not to go back to Herod because Herod wanted to hurt the baby, so they went home a different way.

The magi gave Jesus gifts fit for a king.
What gift would you give baby Jesus?

Matthew 2:1-12

The Flight to Egypt

One night while Joseph was dreaming, God sent an angel to give Joseph a message. The angel said, "Get up! Take Mary and Jesus and go to Egypt. Stay there. Herod wants to kill baby Jesus." While it was still dark, Joseph, Mary and Jesus left their home and ran away to Egypt. It was a long, hard journey.

King Herod didn't know where to find Jesus. He was very angry that the magi, who were supposed to tell him where the baby Jesus was, had disobeyed him. Jesus was safe in Egypt, but Herod was in a rage. Joseph, Mary, and Jesus stayed in Egypt until Herod died.

One night, a messenger from God went to Joseph in a dream. The angel said, "Get up! Take Mary and Jesus, and go back to the land of Israel." Joseph knew God wanted them to live in a safe place, so Joseph and his family went to a town called Nazareth. That's where Jesus grew up.

> Jesus was a child just like you are a child.
> Think of all the things Jesus had to learn as he grew up.

Matthew 2:13-23

Jesus Teaches in the Temple

Jesus grew up in a town called Nazareth. As children do, Jesus grew and changed. He learned to walk and talk, sing and pray. Mary and Joseph loved their son very much and taught Jesus what it means to belong to God. As a family, they worshipped God, prayed, remembered the Ten Commandments, and lived as God wanted them to live.

Mary, Joseph, Jesus, and other Jews went to the city of Jerusalem each year to celebrate the Passover. They remembered how God protected God's people from slavery in Egypt. They praised God for saving them from the waters of the Red Sea, and guiding them to new life in a new homeland.

After the Passover celebration was over, Mary and Joseph began to travel home. They thought Jesus was in the crowd of family and friends who were also going home. At the end of the day, Mary and Joseph searched for Jesus and couldn't find him. Mary and Joseph turned around and went back to Jerusalem to find Jesus. After three days they found Jesus in the temple, teaching the teachers! Everyone was amazed at how much he understood about God and God's way.

When Mary found her son she said, "We've been looking for you! We were so worried! Why did you do this?" Jesus answered, "Why were you looking? Didn't you know that I would be in my Father's house?" Mary and Joseph didn't understand what Jesus meant. Mary, Joseph, and Jesus went home to Nazareth. Jesus grew and grew and became wiser and wiser.

Should Jesus have stayed behind in the temple without telling his parents? How so?

Luke 2:41-52

John Baptizes People

Jesus had a cousin named John, who was the son of Elizabeth and Zechariah. John lived in the wilderness. He ate grasshoppers and honey, and wore scratchy clothes made out of camel hair.

John was a prophet who told people, "Get ready for God to come. Prepare the way!" John reminded people of the prophet Isaiah, from a long time ago before John was born. Isaiah had said, "Take comfort! Prepare! Get ready for what God is doing. Prepare the way!" Isaiah gave beautiful speeches; he said, "Make every road smooth and straight. Lift up low places, and level out high places. Then everyone will see the glory of God!" John spoke like this too.

John knew that in order to be ready for God, people needed to repent; they had to change their ways and live as God wanted them to live. John baptized people in the Jordan River so they would be clean, inside and out, changed and ready to live in new ways for God. People called him "John the Baptizer" or "John the Baptist." John knew that the Messiah, the leader God's people were waiting for was coming. John said, "I baptize you with water, but someone is coming who will be more powerful than I am. He will baptize you with the Holy Spirit." The people waited, watched, and hoped.

Imagine you were having lunch with John. What would you ask him? Would you bring a bag lunch, or would you join him for grasshoppers and honey?

Isaiah 40 • Matthew 3:1-12 • Mark 1:1-8 • Luke 3:1-18 • John 1:19-28

Jesus Is Baptized

Many people from all around the region went to the Jordan River so John the Baptist could baptize them. They confessed their sin—they admitted the wrong things they did and the right things they did not do and they set out to fix them. They heard John preach, "If you have two coats, give one away to someone who needs it. If you have food to eat, share it with someone who is hungry." John's words were interesting, and the people were excited. They wondered what God was going to do.

When Jesus was about 30 years old, it was time for him to begin his important work for God, called his "ministry." Jesus knew he needed to start his ministry by being baptized, so Jesus went to the Jordan River and asked John the Baptist to baptize him. John said, "Why would I baptize you? You should be baptizing me!" Jesus answered, "Do it. This is the right way for me to begin God's work." John agreed and baptized Jesus.

When Jesus came up from the water, the people who were there saw a dove and they heard God say to Jesus, "You are my son. I love you. You please me."

Why do you imagine John didn't think he should baptize Jesus?

Luke 3:10-11 • Matthew 3:13-17

The Devil Tempts Jesus

After Jesus was baptized, God directed him to go into the wilderness. Jesus stayed alone in the wilderness for forty days with no food. He was hungry. He was lonely. While Jesus was in the wilderness, the devil—the voice that tells us to do wrong things—tempted Jesus. The devil said that Jesus should make life easier for himself. The devil tempted Jesus to get more power for himself rather than to use his power to help people.

The devil said, "You are hungry. Make bread out of these stones." Jesus said, "No! Scripture says people need more than bread. They also need God's word."

Again the devil said, "Jump down from the temple. Ask God to save you." Jesus said, "No! Scripture says not to test God but to trust God."

Yet again, the devil said, "If you worship me and not God, I will put you in charge of every country in the world." Jesus said, "No! Scripture says to worship only God."

The devil was strong, but Jesus was stronger. Jesus didn't do the wrong things the devil wanted him to do. Instead, Jesus did what God wanted him to do. Jesus was faithful to God and God's way. Then the devil left, and God's angels came to help Jesus.

What do you do when you are tempted to do wrong things?

Matthew 4:1-11
Mark 1:12-13
Luke 4:1-13

Jesus Calls Followers

Jesus' important work, his ministry, had begun. There was so much to do! Jesus needed helpers.

One day Jesus walked along the Sea of Galilee. He saw two brothers, Peter and Andrew. They were fishing. Jesus said, "Follow me! Rather than catching fish you will catch people!" Right away they dropped their fishing nets and followed Jesus.

Jesus continued his walk along the shore. Then he saw two more brothers, James and John, who were with their father, Zebedee, fixing their nets. Jesus called to them too, "Come, follow me!" James and John got out of their boat, left their father, and followed Jesus.

In all Jesus called twelve people to join his work; they were called disciples. Their names were Peter, Andrew, James, John, another James, Matthew, Thomas, Philip, Bartholomew, Simon, Judas, and Thaddeus. These twelve disciples left everything behind to follow Jesus. They traveled with Jesus and learned how to live in God's way. As they traveled and taught, many other people became Jesus' followers too.

The first disciples were good at fishing. Jesus needed them to keep fishing, but fish in new ways. What are you good at doing? How might you help Jesus with what you do?

Matthew 4:18-22
Mark 1:16-20
Luke 5:1-11

Jesus Performs a Miracle in Cana

One day, Jesus and his mother, Mary, were at a wedding celebration in the town of Cana. The disciples were also at the party. After a while, there wasn't enough wine for everyone to drink. Mary said to Jesus, "They have no wine." She knew her son could help, and she told the servants, "Do whatever he tells you." Jesus pointed to six large stone jars, and he told the servants to fill them with water. Then Jesus said to take some water out of the jars and bring it to the head waiter who tasted it.

The head waiter was surprised. It was not water! It was wine! The head waiter brought the wine to the groom and said, "Usually people serve the best wine first. But you kept the best wine until last when the party is almost over." The wedding guests at the party had more wine than they could possibly drink.

Changing water into wine was Jesus' first miracle. It was amazing! It showed the disciples that Jesus could do what other people can't do. The disciples knew that God was with Jesus.

People can't change water into wine as Jesus did. What can you do that Jesus could do?

John 2:1-11

Jesus Heals a Man

One day Jesus was in a village called Capernaum. Many people wanted to see him, so they crowded into the house where he was. Jesus said such interesting, important things!

Some men came to the house carrying a friend who could not walk or move his body, because he was paralyzed. They knew Jesus could help their friend, but the house was so crowded they could not get his attention.

The men didn't give up. They were sure Jesus could help their friend, so they did something surprising. They climbed up onto the roof and moved some tiles to make a hole. Then the men lowered their friend on his mat through the roof. Down, down the man went until he was by Jesus! Jesus could see the great faith of the man's friends. Jesus said, "Friend, your sins are forgiven."

Some religious leaders were concerned. "God is the only one who can forgive sins." Jesus said, "Which is easier? To forgive a person's sins or to heal someone?" Of course, Jesus could do both of these—forgive and heal. Jesus said to the man, "Stand up, and take your mat and go home." He did! The man was healed. Everyone was amazed and praised God.

Could the man who was paralyzed have been healed without his friends? How so?

Mark 2:1-12
Luke 5:17-26

Jesus Preaches on a Mountain

Wherever Jesus went, people followed him. Young people, old people, and those in between wanted to listen to Jesus because he had such important ideas. Jesus told everyone that God loved them. Jesus helped people know God so they could live as God wanted them to live.

One day a crowd of people was gathered around Jesus. There were so many people! To help everyone see him, Jesus went up a mountain and preached a sermon. In his sermon, Jesus said people are blessed when they know they are loved by God. From the mountainside, Jesus preached:

"People who are poor are blessed by God. They belong to God!
People who are very unhappy are loved by God. They will be comforted!
People who are hungry for the world to match God's way are blessed. They will be filled!
People who care for others are appreciated by God. They will receive care from God!
People whose hearts are like God's heart are blessed. They will see God!
People who make peace are blessed. They will be called God's children!
People who are treated badly when they do the right thing are loved by God. They are part of God's Way!
Rejoice! Be glad!"

Peace means everyone having enough to eat. Peace means everyone being safe. What else does peace mean?

Matthew 5:1-12
Luke 6:12-31

Jesus Tells Stories

Jesus told parables—short stories to help people learn important ideas. When he told parables, Jesus talked about sheep and coins, parents and children, lamps, pearls, and seeds. He talked about yeast for bread, grape vines, treasures, servants, workers, and guests. Jesus used these ordinary things in his parables, but the ideas in his parables are more than ordinary! Each parable is filled with questions to wonder about—over and over again.

Once Jesus asked himself, "What is God's way like? What story can I tell you to help you learn?" He got an idea and told a parable: "Think about what happens when a mustard seed is planted in the ground. It starts out as a tiny seed, but then it grows and grows and grows. It grows larger than any other plants in the garden. It grows so big that birds can make nests in its branches."

This story about the mustard seed is a parable about God's way. God's way is like that mustard seed. It starts out very small, but it grows and keeps growing until it is big and strong—big enough for people to see and strong enough to support life.

Keep thinking about this mustard seed. Be creative. What do you hear Jesus saying in this parable?

Think of your favorite story. What lesson have you learned from it? How do stories teach?

Matthew 13:31-32
Mark 4:30-32
Luke 13:18-19

Jesus Blesses Children

Jesus and the disciples traveled from town to town, they talked to people about God and God's way. They told people that God loves them. They explained that God forgives them when they do wrong things and when they don't do right things, and never stops loving them. It was such good news! People were eager to listen. They wanted to be close to Jesus. They wanted to listen to Jesus.

One day some people brought their children to Jesus. They wanted Jesus to hold them and pray for them. But the disciples thought the children would bother Jesus, so they said, "Stop!" Jesus heard the disciples and he said, "Let the children come! Don't stop them!" Jesus picked up the children, held them in his arms, and he blessed them. Jesus said, "Unless you are like these little children, you will not belong in God's way."

God's way is for people who are like children: creative, joyful, and full of love. These are the ones who will belong and fit right in when things are as God wants them to be.

How does it feel when adults don't have time for children?

Matthew 19:13-15
Mark 10:13-16
Luke 18:15-17

Transfiguration

One day Jesus took his disciples Peter, James, and John, and hiked up a mountain where they could be alone. Right in front of them, Jesus changed completely. His face was bright like the sun, and his clothes were dazzling white. Then Moses and the prophet Elijah appeared beside him, and they talked with Jesus. It was wonderful and mysterious! It was so exciting to be there that Peter said, "Teacher! I will make three tents: one for you, one for Moses, and one for Elijah. Then we can stay here."

As Peter was talking, a cloud settled over the mountain and a voice said, "This is my son. I love him. Listen to him." The disciples fell to the ground in fear. But Jesus touched them and said, "Get up. Don't be afraid." The disciples looked around and now everything looked the same. It was surprising.

As Jesus, Peter, James, and John hiked down the mountain, Jesus told the disciples not to tell anyone what they had seen and heard.

This story reminds us of Jesus' baptism when God also said, "You are my son. I love you." Find a reminder of Jesus' baptism in the art.

Matthew 17:1-9
Mark 9:2-9
Luke 9:28-36

Mary and Martha Learn from Jesus

Jesus and his disciples traveled to many villages teaching people about God. Jesus sat down and ate meals with all kinds of people. Jesus healed people who were sick. Jesus told stories about what it means to live in God's way. Jesus spent time with children, women, and men; everyone was important to Jesus.

Once, Jesus went to a house and visited two sisters who were his friends. The sisters were named Mary and Martha. Martha welcomed Jesus into their home, then she hurried about the house to make sure Jesus was comfortable. Meanwhile, Mary sat at Jesus' feet and listened to him talk. Martha was worried about all the work she had left to do. She said to Jesus, "Teacher, don't you care that Mary has left me to do the work alone? Tell her to help me!"

Jesus answered, "Oh, Martha. You are concerned about many things, but only one thing is important. Mary has chosen the best thing to do." Even though working hard is important, Jesus also wants people to sit and carefully listen.

Does it seem fair to you that Martha worked while Mary listened?

Luke 10:38-42

Jesus Talks with a Samaritan Woman

Jesus and the disciples traveled through a town called Sychar in the region of Samaria. Jesus was tired and the sun was hot. He sat down to rest beside a well while the disciples went to buy some food.

A woman came to get water from the well. Jesus asked, "Could you please give me a drink of water?" The woman was perplexed. Usually Jews like Jesus wouldn't have anything to do with Samaritans like her, because Jews and Samaritans didn't trust each other in those days.

But Jesus was different. He said to the woman, "I am trying to give you water that is full of life." Now the woman was even more perplexed. She said, "Sir, you don't even have a bucket. How can you offer me water?"

Jesus answered, "Everyone who drinks water from a well will be thirsty again. I will give you a different kind of water that flows from a special fountain to give you life." The woman said, "Please give me a drink of that kind of water!"

Jesus and the woman kept talking and listening to each other. The woman was amazed at what Jesus said. She ran to town saying, "Come and see this man! Could he be the messiah we have waited for?"

Many people listened to the woman. They wanted to hear more, so Jesus stayed two more days. When Jesus left, they said, "Now we have seen Jesus for ourselves and we know he will save the world!"

When Jesus was your age, Samaritans were often ignored. What does it feel like to be ignored?

John 4:1-42

Jesus Feeds a Crowd

Jesus and his disciples hiked up a mountain near the Sea of Galilee. Many people followed him because they saw how Jesus healed people who were sick. They were curious.

When Jesus noticed how many people followed them, he said to his disciple Philip, "Where will we get enough food to feed all these people?" Philip answered, "Someone would have to work for half a year to earn enough money to buy bread for this many people!" Another disciple, Andrew, spoke up: "There is a boy here who has five small loaves of bread and two fish. But how could that help with all these people?" After all, there were more than 5,000 people.

Jesus took the bread and gave thanks to God. Then he passed out the bread and the fish. It was amazing! Everyone had plenty to eat. When the disciples gathered up what was left over, there was enough to fill twelve large baskets.

The people knew they had seen a miracle. They looked at Jesus and said, "This must be the one we have been waiting for!" But Jesus wanted to be alone, so he went off by himself.

Do you think this story is about having little or having much? How so?

John 6:1-14

Zacchaeus Meets Jesus

Jesus was going through a city called Jericho. A man named Zacchaeus lived there. Zacchaeus' job was to collect taxes, the money people owned to the government. Zacchaeus was very rich, so people didn't trust him because they wondered if he kept some of the money for himself.

Many people wanted to see Jesus while he was in Jericho, including Zacchaeus. But Zacchaeus was quite short and could not see over the crowd. Zacchaeus got an idea. He climbed a sycamore tree.

When Jesus got to the tree, he looked up and saw Zacchaeus. He said, "Zacchaeus, hurry down! I want to stay with you at your house." Zacchaeus was happy. He climbed down from the tree and welcomed Jesus into his home.

But other people in town grumbled. They said, "Zacchaeus is a sinner! He does not do what God wants. Why is Jesus going to his house?" But Zacchaeus decided to change his ways. He said, "Teacher, I will give half of what I own to people who are poor. And I will pay back the people I have cheated."

Jesus said, "You were lost, but now you and the people in your family have been found." Jesus came to help everyone who needed to find their way to God. Then Jesus and his disciples headed toward Jerusalem.

Do you think Zacchaeus changed for one day or forever?

Luke 19:1-10

The Parade into Jerusalem

Jesus and his disciples were on their way to Jerusalem. When they got close to a place called the Mount of Olives (it was a hill where many olive trees grew), Jesus told two disciples to go into a village and find a young donkey. Jesus said, "Bring the donkey to me. If anyone asks why you are doing this, answer 'The teacher needs it.' They will understand."

The disciples did as Jesus asked. They brought the donkey to Jesus and put their cloaks on the animal's back like a saddle. Jesus sat on the donkey and rode down the path from the Mount of Olives into Jerusalem. Crowds of people saw him. They cheered and shouted for joy. They were so excited! The people waved palms and cried out, "Hosanna! Hooray! Blessed is the One who comes in God's name." There was a lot of happy noise.

Some religious leaders did not like the noise. They said to Jesus, "Teacher, order the people to be quiet." Jesus answered, "I cannot do that. Even if the people were quiet, the stones would shout for them with the same enthusiasm."

If Jesus came to your town, how would you welcome him?

Luke 19:29-40
Matthew 21:1-11

Jesus Turns over Tables

Jesus went to the temple in Jerusalem. The temple was a place to pray, worship, and come close to God. At the temple, Jesus saw people buying and selling doves to use as offerings to God. Other people were changing Roman coins into Jewish coins. The temple was like a marketplace! The people seemed more concerned about business than about God.

Jesus was angry and took action. He turned over the moneychangers' tables. He pushed over the chairs belonging to people selling doves. Jesus said, "Don't you remember? The prophets already told you what God wants for the temple! They said, 'My house is a place for everyone to pray.' But you have turned it into a place where robbers go. This is not what the temple is supposed to be."

When the temple leaders heard what Jesus had done, they were concerned. They did not like what Jesus was saying and teaching. They did not like that Jesus disrupted the way things were. They especially did not like that crowds of people listened to Jesus and agreed with him. The leaders wanted the people on their side, agreeing with them. They wondered if Jesus should go away forever. They made a plan.

> **It is important to be angry in some situations. What makes you angry?**

Mark 11:15-18

One Last Supper

Many leaders were angry with Jesus. They did not like that people listened so carefully to what Jesus said. The leaders wanted to find Jesus and arrest him, so that people would stop following his ways. Judas Iscariot, one of Jesus' disciples, decided to help them. Judas went to the leaders and asked, "What will you give me if I show you where Jesus is? I will betray him for you." The temple leaders agreed to give Judas silver coins if he took them to Jesus.

It was almost time for the Passover celebration, a festival to remember that long ago God saved the people who passed through the Red Sea. Jesus sent Peter and John to prepare the special Passover meal. That night, Jesus and the disciples ate, celebrated, prayed, and thanked God for the Passover. Judas Iscariot was there too.

While they were eating, Jesus took bread, gave God thanks, and said, "Eat this bread. It is my body." Then Jesus took the cup, gave God thanks, and said, "Drink this. This is my blood. Do this to remember me." The disciples were confused. What could all this mean? They became even more confused when Jesus said, "One of you will betray me."

When people betray others, they are don't live up to others' trust. Which would be worse: to be betrayed by someone close to you or betrayed someone you don't know? How so?

Matthew 26:1-5, 14-30
Mark 14:1-2; 10-26
Luke 22:1-20

Jesus Washes the Disciples' Feet

While everyone was eating, Jesus got up from the table. He wrapped a towel around his waist. He put water into a bowl. Then Jesus started washing his disciples' feet. He dried their feet with the towel. Jesus did this to express his love to the disciples and to show them how to love and care for each other.

When Jesus got to Peter, he said, "Are you going to wash my feet?" Jesus said, "I know you don't understand what I am doing, but later you will." Peter said, "Oh no! You will never wash my feet!" Jesus answered, "If I don't wash your feet, you won't belong to me." Jesus washed all the disciples' feet, even Judas' feet.

When Jesus was done, he sat down again at the table. He asked, "Do you understand what I have done? I have given you an example of how you should live and love each other. When you do the things I have done, and love as I have loved, God will be with you."

Why do you think Peter did not want Jesus to wash his feet?

John 13:1-16

Jesus Prays in a Garden

When the meal was over, Jesus and the disciples sang a song. They walked out of Jerusalem to a hill where many olive trees grew. It was called The Mount of Olives.

Jesus said to the disciples, "All of you will run away and leave me alone tonight." Peter answered, "No! I will never, ever leave you." The other disciples said they would never abandon Jesus either.

On the Mount of Olives, Jesus and the disciples went into a garden called Gethsemane.

Jesus said, "I am feeling sad and alone. Please stay awake to keep me company. I am going to go pray." Jesus walked a little farther. He was extremely upset. Jesus prayed to God, "Please stop what is going to happen to me. But if this is what has to happen, I will do it."

It was evening and the disciples were tired. While Jesus prayed, they fell asleep.

Jesus returned to the disciples and saw them sleeping. He said to Peter, "You're sleeping?! Can't you even stay awake for one hour?" For a second time, Jesus went to another part of the garden and prayed, and again the disciples fell asleep. Then for a third time, Jesus prayed and the disciples slept again.

The disciples were tired. Was it right for them to sleep even though Jesus asked them to stay awake? Why was it important to Jesus for them to stay awake?

Matthew 26:36-46
Mark 14:32-42
Luke 22:39-46

Jesus Is Betrayed and Arrested

After Jesus finished praying, he was still very, very upset. It was late in the evening, and he felt lonely because the disciples who were with him kept falling asleep. But the disciples didn't know why Jesus was so upset.

While they were still in the garden named Gethsemane, on the Mount of Olives, Judas Iscariot came to the garden with soldiers following him. Judas had already decided to betray Jesus by helping the people who wanted Jesus to stop teaching people about God's way. Judas told the soldiers as they went into the garden, "The one I kiss is Jesus, the man you want to arrest."

Jesus loved Judas. Jesus ate with Judas. Jesus washed Judas' feet. Jesus shared bread and the cup with Judas. Jesus trusted Judas. So when Judas greeted him and kissed him, Jesus didn't try to run away.

Immediately the soldiers arrested Jesus, and the disciples ran away.

Why do you think the disciples ran away?
Does it surprise you that they ran away? How so?

Matthew 26:47-56
Mark 14:43-50
Luke 22:47-54
John 18:1-8

The Crucifixion

After Jesus was arrested, many people wanted him dead. The religious leaders had a meeting. They decided to take Jesus to Pontius Pilate, the government's leader. Pilate listened to their complaints about Jesus, but he did not think Jesus had done anything wrong. Pilate thought the temple leaders were jealous. But many people began to shout, "Crucify Jesus! Crucify him!" They wanted Jesus to be gone forever.

Pilate did what the people wanted. He ordered the soldiers to beat Jesus and nail him on a cross. Soldiers put sharp thorns on Jesus' head like a crown. They put Jesus' cross between two men who were also hung on crosses to die because they had broken the law. Jesus cried out, "God, why have you forgotten me?" Jesus also said, "Forgive the ones who did this to me. They don't know what they are doing." Then at noon, darkness covered everything, even the sun, and it stayed dark for three hours. Jesus died.

A soldier who watched Jesus die said, "This man belonged to God!" Later that day, they took Jesus' body down from the cross and gave it to a man named Joseph from Arimathea. Joseph wrapped Jesus' body in cloth and laid him in a tomb. They rolled a heavy rock in front of the tomb.

Jesus' mother, Mary, and Jesus' followers wept. Their hope for everything to be new and different died with Jesus.

When Jesus died, the whole land was covered in darkness. What does darkness feel like?

Matthew 27 •
Mark 15 •
Luke 23 •
John 18:28-19:42

The Women Visit the Tomb

Early in the morning before sunrise, Mary Magdalene and some other women went to Jesus' tomb. They were bringing spices, like perfume, to put on Jesus' dead body as people did in those days.

They wondered, "How will we get into the tomb? Who will roll away the stone?" When they got to the tomb, the stone was already moved. They walked in and were afraid. They saw someone dressed in white who said, "Don't be afraid. You are looking for Jesus who was crucified. Look! He is not here. He has been raised to new life! Now, go and tell Jesus' disciples the good news!"

The eleven disciples could not believe the good news the women told them. They thought it sounded like a made-up story. Peter wanted to see for himself, so he went to the tomb and looked in. He saw the cloth that Jesus' body had been wrapped in, but Jesus' body was gone. Peter went home amazed by what had happened.

Why do you think the women were afraid? Is it possible to be afraid and happy at the same time?

Matthew 28:1-10
Mark 16:1-8
Luke 24:1-12

A Walk to Emmaus

On the same day Jesus was raised to new life, two of Jesus' followers were walking to a village called Emmaus.

As they walked, they talked about Jesus and how he had died on the cross. While they were talking, Jesus came and started walking with them, but the travelers didn't recognize him. Jesus said, "What are you talking about?"

One follower named Cleopas answered, "You must be the only person who isn't talking about what happened in Jerusalem!"

"What do you mean?" Jesus said.

The two travelers said, "We thought Jesus was the one we had been waiting for to save Israel, but then he was arrested and crucified. Now some women in our group say that an angel told them Jesus is alive. We don't know what to think."

As they entered Emmaus, the travelers said, "It's getting late. Come stay with us." Jesus did.

When they were eating, Jesus took bread, blessed it, and broke it. Immediately the travelers knew it was Jesus! But as soon as they recognized him, Jesus vanished. They left right away for Jerusalem to tell everyone else that Jesus came to them in the breaking of the bread.

If you could talk and walk with Jesus, what would you talk about?

Luke 24:13-35

Thomas Sees Jesus

A week after Jesus rose from the dead, the disciples were together in a house.

It was a secret meeting, and all the doors were locked. Suddenly Jesus came and stood with the disciples. He greeted them saying, "Peace be with you."

A disciple named Thomas was confused. Thomas hadn't seen Jesus since the crucifixion, and he didn't understand how Jesus could live again. Jesus held out his hands so Thomas could see the scars from the nails. Jesus said to Thomas, "Look at me. Put your finger here. Touch my side. It's me. Believe." Thomas answered, "My teacher and my God!"

Jesus said, "Thomas, do you believe because you have seen me? From now on, people who come later will be able to believe too. They will be blessed." Jesus knew that people who lived after Thomas would not see him directly, but they would still know Jesus because Thomas saw for them.

Jesus appeared to his disciples many times after he rose from the dead. He ate with them. He told people to love as he loved. He called people to follow him. Jesus did so many things that if they were all written down, there would not be room in the world to hold all the books.

We don't know if Thomas touched Jesus or not.
What do you think?

John 20:19-29
John 21:25

Jesus Goes to Heaven

Jesus did not stay on the earth forever. For forty days after he had risen from the tomb and God gave him new life, Jesus spent time with his disciples. Jesus taught them. He ate with them. He told them about God and how God wants things to be. Jesus said, "Soon you will receive power from the Holy Spirit. Then you will be able to tell people all over the world about me and the way of God. Tell everyone!"

When Jesus finished talking and the people were watching, something mysterious happened. Jesus was lifted up and a cloud came over him so no one could see him with their eyes any longer. Jesus had returned to be completely with God forever.

The people were still looking up when suddenly two people wearing white robes stood by them. They said, "Why are you looking toward heaven? Someday Jesus will return where you are."

Jesus' followers went back to Jerusalem. They joined the eleven disciples, some women, and Jesus' brothers and mother. Together they worshipped and prayed.

What would you like to be doing when Jesus comes back?

Acts 1:1-11

The Pentecost Celebration

For the festival of Pentecost, Jews from all around the world were in Jerusalem. They celebrated God giving Moses the Ten Commandments. Jesus' followers were there too, gathered together in one house. Suddenly there was a great gust of wind that came from heaven. Then flames of fire danced over each one of them. It was the Holy Spirit! With the Holy Spirit, each disciple was able to speak a different language, but still they could understand each other. It was amazing and the people were puzzled. "What does this mean?" they wondered.

Peter stood up and said, "God has given us the power of the Holy Spirit, so we can tell you that Jesus, who was crucified, has been raised to new life. He is the Messiah, the new leader God promised."

When the crowd heard this, they asked, "What should we do?" Peter answered, "Change your ways. Be baptized. Live as God wants you to live. God will give you the Holy Spirit. This promise is for you, your children, and all those near and far. It is a promise for everyone."

It is a wonderful promise.

What can you tell others about Jesus and God's way?

Acts 2:1-41

People of the Way: Let Justice Roll

After flames danced over Jesus' followers at Pentecost, and the Holy Spirit gave them power and courage, they said to one another, "We have good news to share!" and they started telling other people about Jesus and about God's way. Many people listened, and now there were even more followers. These followers prayed together. They ate together. They shared bread with each other. They called themselves "People of the Way."

These followers remembered that Amos, a prophet, said, "God wants justice to be like a waterfall, strong and free. God wants goodness to be like a stream that never ends."

Sometimes the people were confused about what God wanted them to do, but they recalled that a prophet named Micah said, "Don't be confused about what God wants. Remember: Do what is right and fair! Be kind! Walk humbly in God's way!"

And followers remembered that Jesus said, "When you love each other, I am with you." Back then and still today, followers believe that Jesus—who died and rose to new life—is there when they feed people who are hungry, give water to people who are thirsty, visit people who are lonely, and show love, forgiveness, and grace.

May it be so. Amen.

This book ends, but the story continues when people follow the way of God. What will you do? How will you live?

Acts 2:43-47
Amos 5:21-24
Micah 6:1-8
Matthew 25:31-46

A Note to Adults

The stories in this book are from long ago and far away, yet they are also our stories. They tell us who we are. They show us who God is. They give us an invitation to live in God's way. Please read the stories in this book over and over again with the children in your life. In its pages you will find ideas and images to last a lifetime.

Learning the Biblical Story

The Bible is at the center of Christianity. It records the long, complicated, holy relationship between God, the world, and people. Within its pages we find:

- stories of beginnings;
- stories of people finding their way, figuring out what it means to belong to God;
- stories of brave people who make mistakes;
- stories of God's never-ending promises;
- stories of despair, doubt and confusion;
- stories of joy, conviction and determination;
- stories of ruthless rulers;
- stories of surprising people God raises up as leaders;
- stories of Jesus, God-made-human, living among people just like us;
- stories of Jesus' life—a life of love, grace and forgiveness;
- stories of people who first experienced Jesus as the Christ, the living and breathing fulfillment of God's promises, God's lasting answer to human destruction.

Taken together, these stories show us who God is, what it means to live in God's way, and what discipleship is all about.

If you want to read more about these stories in the Bible, each *Picture the Bible* story shows you where to look by listing the book name, chapter number, and verses where the story is found in the Bible. It looks like this, for example: Acts 2:1-41 (which means, turn to the book of Acts in the Bible, find chapter 2 in Acts, and read verses 1-41 of chapter 2). Sometimes the biblical reference doesn't include verses, like this: Jonah 1–4 (which means, find the book of Jonah in the Bible and read chapters 1 through 4).

Picture the Bible is filled with 52 individual narratives that together represent the grand biblical story, from the Creation to the beginning of the Church. The narrative in *Picture the Bible*:

- stays close to the biblical text;
- presents stories with careful paraphrases to engage readers of all ages;
- uses inclusive language for God and people;
- invites readers to hear individual stories alone but also weaves them together, showing God's long relationship with the creation and human family.

Picture the Bible is for people of all ages. Read it by yourself, as families, and as members of the body of Christ. Talk about the question included with each story. Look up and read the larger biblical narrative surrounding each image. Jump into these stories. Let them mold and shape you.

Engaging the Art

The collages in *Picture the Bible* provide enough detail to convey the respective stories, but are not so symbolic that interpretation is overly complicated. The intent is for the images to become readily embedded in readers' imaginations. The art in *Picture the Bible*:

- draws people into the image so viewers can imagine themselves in the story;
- reflects the tremendous variety among God's people;
- are original collages from the private collection of First Congregational Church in River Falls, Wisconsin;
- were created by artists Amy Sands, Jacqueline Lakely, and Kathryn Brewer.

Picture the Bible was originally conceived to encourage biblical literacy and interpretation. To experience the art in its fullness, engage children in conversations similar to the following:

- What do you notice first in the picture? What else do you see?
- What colors do you see? Can you find more than one shade of a particular color?
- Use words to retell the story in the picture.
- Who are the people in the picture? What are they doing?
- Look at the lines in the picture. Are they curly or straight? Find a straight line and trace it with your finger. Find a curvy line and trace it with a different finger.
- Use words to describe the picture's feelings.
- Pretend you are standing in this picture. What sounds would you hear?
- Find a picture of surprise. A picture of fear. A picture of joy. A picture of expectation.
- Find your favorite picture/story. What makes it your favorite?

Final Words

Be curious about these stories. Ask questions about them. Wonder what they teach you and prompt you to do. Grow in faithfulness so through you, others will know God and God's way. My hope is for all God's children see themselves in this art and these stories and embrace the call to live in God's way—
a way of justice, love, forgiveness, hope, and grace. *Soli Deo gloria.*

—Stacy Johnson Myers

Artist Credits

Amy Sands

God Makes the World
Adam and Eve in the Garden
Jealousy and Murder
The Big Flood
God's Promise to Abraham and Sarah
Joseph and his Brothers
Living in Slavery
God Speaks to Moses
The Ten Commandments
A New Homeland
God Chooses David
Sent Away to Babylon
Isaiah's Message
God Chooses Mary
Jesus Is Born
Jesus Teaches in the Temple
John Baptizes People
Jesus Is Baptized
The Devil Tempts Jesus
Jesus Calls Followers
Jesus Performs a Miracle in Cana
Jesus Heals a Man
Jesus Preaches on a Mountain
Jesus Tells Stories
Jesus Blesses Children
Transfiguration
The Parade into Jerusalem
One Last Supper
Jesus Washes the Disciples' Feet
The Crucifixion
The Women Visit the Tomb
A Walk to Emmaus
Thomas Sees Jesus
Jesus Goes to Heaven
The Pentecost Celebration

Jacqueline Lakely

Baby Moses
The Passover
Fleeing from Egypt
King Solomon's Temple
Naaman is Healed
Daniel and the Lions
Jonah and the Big Fish
The Magi Visit Jesus
The Flight to Egypt
Mary and Martha Learn from Jesus
Jesus Talks with a Samaritan Woman
Jesus Feeds a Crowd
Zacchaeus Meets Jesus
Jesus Turns over Tables
Jesus Prays in a Garden
Jesus Is Betrayed and Arrested

Kathryn Brewer

People of the Way: Let Justice Roll

Kathryn Brewer also served as art director for *Picture the Bible*.

Reproductions of the art and additional *Picture the Bible* resources are available at www.picturethebible.org.